# BUYER LEGENDS

# BUYER LEGENDS

## THE EXECUTIVE STORYTELLER'S GUIDE

BRYAN & JEFFREY EISENBERG
WITH ANTHONY GARCIA

Text copyright © 2014 Bryan & Jeffrey Eisenberg with Anthony Garcia

No part of this book may be reproduced, or stored in a retrieval system, or transmitted in any form or by any means, electronic, mechanical, photocopying, recording, or otherwise, without express written permission of the publisher.

ISBN-13: 9781502757654

# INTRODUCTION

In just under 20 years, Amazon has become a legendary brand. By managing the metrics that align with their brand story, Amazon offers great selection, availability, price, and an always-improving buying experience. However, this data-centric approach is not the secret to their brand and management success.

Did you know that Jeff Bezos, in place of PowerPoint presentations in meetings, requires his execs to write six-page narrative memos?

Did you know that before an Amazon product is even developed, the product manager is required to write a press release for that proposed product?

The little understood secret is that Amazon starts each business initiative with a narrative, and the clarity and understanding derived from those narratives disseminates to all levels of the company and keeps every channel and customer experience congruent.

### Left brain/Right brain

Stories that cannot be measured are creative fiction. Buyer Legends bind business metrics to what the customer experiences.

Another company that has found success using a similar technique is Airbnb. By using narrative along with storyboards, Airbnb has managed to accelerate growth and build a strong up-and-coming brand without spending money on advertising. "Building a strong story and brand comes from paying attention to all those details that make up the whole experience for users," says Joe Gebbia, one of the Founders of Airbnb.

Buyer Legends make use of narratives to help your marketing and sales teams map and improve the customers' shopping and buying journeys. Buyer Legends amplify your brand story from a simple tale into a legend. With the right legend, more prospects turn into buyers, and more observers of your brand become believers. Indeed, the problem with most brand stories is that they're told by the wrong people. For a brand story to work, it has to be told by all employees and customers, both to themselves and each other.

More practically, Buyer Legends is the process of using narratives and storytelling in your marketing and selling efforts. By writing stories, or Buyer Legends, about how your customers interact with your brand, you and your company will better understand your customers and have a 'legend' you can use to map more compelling customer experiences.

## The Competitive Advantage of Buyer Legends

- **Improve communications.** Your whole team will see and understand the bigger picture
- **Improve execution.** You will turn big directives into purposeful and more effective actions
- **Improve testing.** You will understand how to plan and implement more effective tests
- **Make more money.** You will see improved conversion rates that make the up-front planning worth the time and effort

After reading this, you will have more insight as to why your marketing execution may not be meeting expectations and why your team might be struggling to "get it." You will begin to see how the Buyer Legends process IS one of the final pieces of a complex puzzle that has been missing from your marketing efforts.

## Why Smart Marketers Get Mediocre Results from Great Tools - A Marketer's Story

> Wading through the login to her campaign dashboards, Gloria holds her breath, then as the familiar screen comes up, she does a double take. Those are way off from previous campaigns! She hops on IM and asks her senior team to come to her office right away.
>
> Poker-faced, Gloria simply stares at her computer and says nothing as arriving team members take seats scattered near her desk. From the corners of her eyes, she can see them subtly fidget and glance at each other for reassurance.

As a CMO, Gloria kept up with the leading edge of marketing strategies. She'd taken time others had suggested was unnecessary to carefully create personas; she'd researched data-driven marketing; she'd put an optimization testing program in place, and even developed a content marketing strategy. Gloria felt certain if she could gather enough tools in her marketing toolbox, at least one would make a substantial impact on her campaign's execution and effectiveness.

## What's in your Marketing toolbox?

- Data-driven Marketing
- Analytics
- Marketing Automation
- Usability and User Experience
- Content Marketing
- Personas
- Testing and Optimization Platforms
- Social Media
- Mobile
- Branding
- Psychology, Human Behavior and Persuasion
- Design and Layout
- Search Marketing and Remarketing
- Email and Display Ads
- Traditional Media
- (Fill in the blank)

If you use only a few or all of them, great! With Buyer Legends, your team will best understand how each of these tools contributes to the customer's experience, making your efforts more powerful.

But if Gloria were honest, they were seeing only modest gains after adopting these strategies and practices, not the dramatically-improved messaging and metrics they'd worked hard and hoped for. Worse, it often felt like her team could never really "own" these marketing practices. They'd use them when directed, but they never became go-to tools that fundamentally changed the way the team thought about marketing.

Then Gloria read about Buyer Legends, a process that promised to bridge the gap between brand story and execution/messaging. At first, Gloria rolled her eyes, thinking that sort of gap-bridging was what personas and testing were supposed to do. But she kept looking into the approach that billed itself as different. It was different. Three advantages set it apart from the rest of the strategy/tactics information swamping her.

1. It would work with the branding work she'd already done.
2. It would make her carefully-created personas more predictive and allow her team to take better-informed actions.
3. It would give her a roadmap of what to test as well as how to interpret those results and what to do with the results.

Gloria had asked her team to experiment with Buyer Legends on the new campaign.

> When the silence in her office seems about to explode, Gloria grins and turns her monitor so the team can see.
> 
> "These are the first numbers for the targeted campaign we launched yesterday." Gloria begins to rattle off some numbers and as the string grows more impressive, she watches the faces around her come alive with surprise, disbelief, and excitement. Her Design Lead lets out a "Whoop!" and raises her arm for a fist bump.
> 
> Gloria stands. "You guys KILLED it!" As everyone gradually calms, she continues, "I know we had some wobbly moments getting this one out, and the Buyer Legends took us a little bit out of our comfort zones. Yeah," she laughs, glancing in a mischievously self-effacing way at two members on her left, "I know you thought I was crazy for questioning some of those best practices to do this, but we knocked this one out of the park! Lunch is on me!!"
> 
> Gloria is one marketer in one particular situation, but most marketers can relate to her frustrations in getting the promised lift from much-touted marketing methods and technologies. We've walked in those shoes.

## Brands Have Stories

Some of those stories are real, some imagined. Customers don't usually hear all of them, some might not believe any of them. But, every time your customers interact with your brand, they begin to create a story of their experience with you.

Your customers are hoping you will delight them. No nuance or detail is neutral. Every click, every conversation, every interaction either enhances the customer experience or detracts from it.

## Buyer Legends Help You Deliver on the Promise of Your Brand

The concept of narrative — story — is increasingly finding its way into the marketing world. We've just told a story about a CMO who used a process to achieve success in a marketing campaign. But Gloria's story isn't the point of this book. The story that matters most is the story that takes place between company and customer.

Without story, data on the actions customers take is just data, more or less static. If you do not understand the context, the story of an interaction between a customer and the brand, you can interpret nothing. Obviously interactions happen between brands and customers all day long, but until now, the tools you have been given to understand those interactions have either focused on the brand (through brand story/branding) or the customer (through personas), not on the decision-making, shopping, and buying experiences that happen between brand and customer.

To understand this dynamic, you need a story.

> "100,000 years of evolutionary reliance on story has built into the human genetic code instructions to wire the brain to think in story terms by birth."
>
> —Dr. Steven Pinker,
> Experimental Psychologist

Humans have only one tool capable of communicating the subjective experience of relationship through time, and that's narrative. Ask someone about a favorite possession, and you'll hear a story. Ask them about a friend or spouse and you'll hear a story. There simply is no other way to talk about relationship. And that goes for the relationship between customer and company (or brand) as well.

Story is at the heart of the business process we call Buyer Legends. Buyer Legends takes the perspective of your customer as they interact with your brand, insuring you are delivering on the promise of your brand story, because the brand story that matters is not the one you want to tell, but the one your customers experience when they engage with you.

# WHAT ARE BUYER LEGENDS?

B uyer Legends is a simple scenario narrative process that helps identify the gap between brand story and buyer experience. If you can see a disconnect between the two, it's easier for you to understand what improvements are necessary and how to take action.

Just as importantly, Buyer Legends insures all business decisions are made directly by the team that is responsible for (owns) the results, not indirectly by the creative, retail, customer service, legal, technology, and/or sales teams.

## Why Marketers Sometimes Fail in Communicating with Their Team

*Steve is the new CEO of a B2B accounting-services company that provides SaaS (software as a service) to mostly small businesses of 100 employees or fewer. The home page was formal and dry with very few images. He wanted to humanize an overly-technical company and the sentence, "Include more faces on our site and our marketing material", was one among several bullet points the CEO had sent in a deck to his execs.*

*Without hesitation, his CMO handed it to the designer, who immediately came up with a few mock-ups. After several iterations, they settled on a design featuring, as the hero image, an attractive, 20-something, blue-eyed blond smiling professionally into the camera.*

> They pushed the new home page live, and within 24 hours conversion on the site had dropped 23 percent. By the second day, it had dropped 36%.
>
> The CMO swiftly ordered user tests to learn what went wrong. Users universally missed the message and the call-to-action because they were distracted by the virtual 'eye contact' with the young woman in the picture. In addition, small business owners could not relate to the college-aged, 24-year-old, and the credibility of the company suffered. The picture was eventually replaced with a picture of a more mature woman whose gaze drew prospects' eyes in the direction of the call-to-action. Nevertheless, too many anxiety-filled cycles were devoted to this issue.

Talented marketing teams execute on directives day in and day out, and in this case they did exactly as they were asked, but they did so without a clear understanding of the context of the CEO's needs.

Even though the bullet point was clear and (seemingly) actionable: "Include more faces on our site and marketing material" it was -- as many bullet points are -- absent of context.

When Steve tasked his team, they were left with little understanding of how these newly included "faces" were supposed to be incorporated into the website, how they were intended to make the customer feel, and in what context the customer would encounter them.

So, they filled those gaps with their own assumptions, many totally at odds with those Steve had when he issued his directive. Not surprisingly, the results were disastrous. And it took quite a few back-and-forths to fix it.

This is the problem with all context-poor communication, not just bullets, though they happen to be the most widely abused offenders. Context-poor statistics (a.k.a. "damned lies"), test results, and best practices can often -- and often have -- misled many a marketer and executive.

## Overcoming Communication Challenges with Narrative

The only way to overcome this is to provide context through story. One champion of this approach is none other than Jeff Bezos, founder and CEO of Amazon.com.

Bezos has tossed aside PowerPoint use in staff meetings and instead requires his senior execs to write 4-to-6-page narrative memos. Each memo must clearly state the challenge and objective, outline the possible solutions, and differentiate the proposed solution from what has already been attempted.

He then begins each meeting with a quiet study time so that all attendees can read the memos before discussing them. This is one important reason Amazon.com is innovating at breakneck speed and delivering a customer experience that is years ahead of its competitors. They are actively writing their history and re-writing their futures in story format prior to making business decisions -- even when, in fact especially when, those decisions are highly data-driven.

What if Steve had distributed a similar narrative memo making the case for a more human and conversational company?

> "After a presentation—63% of attendees remember stories—only 5% remember statistics."
> —Authors, Chip and Dan Heath

Unfortunately, this kind of story or narrative-centric approach is currently a rarity in marketing. Think about it: when was the last time you received customer information, demographics, analytics or even campaign objectives that weren't bullet points? Even if they weren't actually bulleted, chances are they weren't given with any context-rich background narrative to provide you with the critical perspectives and information that made it possible to understand what truly needed doing.

Then we all wonder why so many of our marketing executions fail to reflect our strategic plans, or require so many iterations to get right, or fail to deliver the results we hoped for.

## Research Data Doesn't Bridge the Company/Customer Gap

You are the new CMO for a blue chip company. Sales are down and have been declining for a while. Your product used to be the gold standard of the industry, but marketing tests — not just a few, but lots, conducted over several years — keep showing that customers want exactly what your product isn't known for.

## What do you do?

- Launch a new version of the product with exactly the features your customers are demanding?
- Double down on what your product used to be celebrated for, even though that now seems to be dragging down sales?

If you voted to launch a new version, you're in good company. That's a solid, data-driven decision, one that most other CMOs or even CEOs would make. Data hardly ever contains the answer. However, it is a great tool for asking better questions.

In 1985, Roberto Goizueta, then CEO of The Coca-Cola Company, was grappling with a 15-year downward sales spiral that threatened to make Pepsi the #1 soft drink in America.

What people liked about Pepsi was its sweetness. Test after test showed it. Coke was more refreshing and far less sweet.

So, Roberto launched "New Coke". Many of us remember how that turned out. After a few months, the company was forced to reintroduce "Classic" Coke; "New Coke" became THE classic tale of brand blundering.

In retrospect, it's easy to make fun of a "boneheaded" branding move, but at the time it was a thoroughly tested and data-driven decision. Coca-Cola blind taste-tested their new secret formula on over 200,000 cola connoisseurs, and they'd overwhelmingly chosen it over Classic Coke. None of us run that many tests with this sort of certainty.

So, what was wrong with the tests?

Coca-Cola described it best in a company blog post about the "New Coke" incident.

What these (secret formula blind taste) tests didn't show, of course, was the bond consumers felt with their Coca-Cola — something they didn't want anyone, including The Coca-Cola Company, tampering with.

Analytical tools and research couldn't tell the Coca-Cola execs how Susie, a 36-year-old mother of two, treats herself to a can of ice-cold Coke after working in the garden and the nostalgia it invokes. Nor could they reveal how she sits at her kitchen table and savors every sip as she traces the Coca-Cola letters with her finger through the condensation trickling down the sides of the can. They also didn't mention John, a 44-year-old cab driver in Queens, who has a Sunday night ritual of watching a horror movie, scarfing down a white pizza with a tall glass filled with fizzing Coke and exactly four ice cubes. In other words, the tests didn't tell the executives how their customers had built an identity around "The Real Thing."

You can't devise the tests that could show you the dimensions of customer experience unless you've trained yourself to think in terms of story and to look for context-rich narratives that capture those all-important interactions between customers and brand.

Research, reports, testing, analysis, spreadsheets, graphs, and charts are perfect for measuring and tracking behaviors, charting trends and counting beans. But these tools are ineffective for understanding the motivation, emotions, desires, and preferences of the very thing most important to the company — your customers. In fact, neuroscience research has demonstrated with fMRI studies that when people engage in analytical thought, their ability to empathize is repressed and vice versa.

What if, before conducting all those blind taste tests, Coke executives first sought to understand the story of the customer and her relationship with Coke?

# APPLYING STORYTELLING TO MARKETING

Whether they're hieroglyphics inside the walls of an ancient pyramid, a fairy tale, a novel, or the latest blockbuster movie, we love stories. Stories place us in the hero's shoes and transfer subjective experience, just as if we ourselves had lived it. In stories, toys cannot only come to life, they can make us root for them, cry with them, and laugh with them. And so it is that Pixar can make an animated robot seem as real as the kid sitting next to us in the theater.

Stories do far more than entertain. They are the context for how we connect and understand each other. And they are a powerful means for transferring our experience to someone who hasn't lived it directly.

Stories are the difference between mastering the facts and understanding reality. Our CEO Steve's marketing team knew the demographics of the target audience, because that information was in at least one of the 11, or maybe it was 16, decks they received that month. But what if they had been able to read this "Buyer Legend" of their typical customer?

## A Buyer Legends Sample

> Vince just learned yesterday that Sandy, his bookkeeper of 14 years, is quitting for personal reasons. She'd gone on a two-month leave of absence a few years ago, and it had taken three younger people to semi-competently do her job. A couple of his jeweller friends have suggested he look into an online service to handle his 27-employee payroll.
>
> Vince likes to call the three stores he has built across Houston Metro his 'jewelry store empire". At 46, he is at the top of his business game, but he is also set in his ways, and must be dragged kicking and screaming to the computer and into the Internet Age. Vince opens his laptop with more than a tinge of resentment. It never takes much for him to get flustered when he is online.
>
> As he arrives at Steve's company website, he sees faces like his and reads short testimonials from small business owners. The faces look like the entrepreneurs and business owners he meets and networks with. One of the testimonials tells of a customer's struggle with deployment and how the customer support team worked closely with his staff to fix the problems. Vince is wise enough to know these types of deployments always have problems, and because the testimonials don't seem to cherry-pick perfect customer experiences, his confidence that this company might be a viable option grows.

Not only does this Buyer Legend give Steve's marketing team a clear understanding of what kinds of faces he needs on his marketing content, it also informs the team about other relevant and common customer needs they should be taking into account. Specifically, it describes the state of the technology-averse business owner. It identifies the deep connection a small business owner has with his "baby" and the extent to which he relies on staff who will care as much and give as much as he does. It provides the copywriter guidance on what types of testimonials to feature. If this Buyer Legend — customer story — were to continue, the subsequent narratives that addressed solutions the customer could choose based on feelings of confidence would enable the entire web team to create a customer-centric experience that requires of Vince (and others like him) only minimum and basic interaction with technology while giving him the information he needs to pick up the phone and start a business conversation.

This is simply one among many Buyer Legends. We could construct a Buyer Legend of a young entrepreneur who needs payroll services for his high-tech start up but is extremely concerned with privacy and security. Or we could construct a Buyer Legend, a vivid story, of a compliance-obsessed Executive Assistant who has been tasked with finding online accounting options for the VP of Operations.

## Buyer Legends use techniques from fiction to deliver a delightful reality

Buyer Legends aren't stories randomly plucked from the ether. Buyer Legends are constructed from all those analytical tools like research and analytics. Each Buyer Legend is representative of one or more customer segment and narrates a successful experience between your customer and your company. Legends can tell the story of a customer on your site, a customer engaging a call center or chat, or any type of interaction pre- or post-sale.

Buyer Legends are constructed from real experience as well. From the issues real people face, the goals they hope to solve, from their needs to feel comfortable with the choices they've made. The best Buyer Legends usually contain both data as well as real life experiences from customers or even lost prospects.

"Story, businesses are realizing, means BIG MONEY."
—Daniel Pink,
A Whole New Mind

## Using Buyer Legends for More than Bridging the Customer Experience Gap

Buyer Legends aren't just useful for detailed customer experience planning either. Buyer Legends tell the brand story of a company or product. Consider some of the most powerful brands today. Apple's "Think Different" story has propelled them to create three landscape-changing products and re-define retail sales, e-commerce, and digital media sales. Nike's "Just Do It" stories propelled a simple commodity like footwear into a high dollar statement that tells the world more about the wearer than the shoe itself. Or, think of the DeBeers "A Diamond is Forever" story and how it has turned a jewelry-grade sparkly stone into a romantic necessity that is five times more expensive than its weight in pure gold.

What story is your brand telling? Is it the same story your customers are hearing? What are your customers' stories? How are they experiencing your brand?

"A brand is no longer what we tell consumers it is—
it is what consumers tell each other it is."
—Scott D. Cook,
Founder, Intuit; Board of Directors, P&G

If you overlook and are unable to empathize with your customers - if you can't orchestrate your chapter in the customer stories that happen in and around your brand - you risk having your competitors write their own ending to your story.

## The Marketer's Story Continued: Buyer Legend Pays Off

*Gloria has just gotten back from her celebratory lunch with her senior team. Marta, her junior copywriter, appears at her office door and requests a few minutes of her time. Marta is smart but a little rough around the edges. She always does what is asked of her, but she's never 'wowed' Gloria. Her copy always seems a little 'tinny' to Gloria's ears, and Marta never quite 'gets it' when Gloria tries to coach her. This is the first time she has ever come to Gloria's office voluntarily. Intrigued, Gloria invites Marta to sit down.*

"How can I help you, Marta?"

"I was writing copy for the Getting Started page this morning so I reread Connie's Buyer Legend. You remember, Connie is our 32-year-old Executive Assistant persona."

"The persona who is researching us for her boss right?" Gloria asks.

Marta nods. "And it says her boss is impatient and wants options right away."

"Yeah, I remember."

"The only option Connie has on the Getting Started page is our standard lead form. So it occurred to me that the day or two she has to wait to get some material from Sales might be too long, and her boss's impatience might force her to recommend another company who can answer some of these questions right away."

"You're probably right," Gloria says.

"So, I took a little time to write up the first part of a one-sheet that Connie can download from the page and then print out for her boss. I wanted to show it to you and see what you thought before I spent any more time on it." Marta is now glowing with confidence.

"Marta, this is a great idea!" Gloria takes Marta's proposal and starts to read.

"Stories are the single most powerful weapon in a leader's arsenal."
—Dr. Howard Gardner,
Harvard University

Gloria has to admit Marta is one of the last people on her staff she expected to embrace the Buyer Legends process, but here she is, going above and beyond and finally 'getting it.' She notices even the quality of Marta's writing is better.

*Marta says she has spoken with one of the developers and explained Connie's narrative to him and why this one-sheet will be important to Connie and other customers like her. The developer told her he'd be happy to spend a little time recoding the page, he could easily knock it out in a hour of his own time.*

*"Wow, Marta. Awesome work!"*

*Gloria and her team have found their groove. She takes a moment to savor it. Since she started as the CMO for ACME she has never worked so hard to achieve so few victories. But that is starting to turn around.*

*With things going this well, she chuckles, maybe her Chicago Cubs will win the World Series this year.*

# GETTING STARTED WITH BUYER LEGENDS - PERFECT IS THE ENEMY OF GOOD ENOUGH

Buyer Legends is a tool that any business can use to improve customer experience in a relatively short period of time. And just like a hammer or any other tool, you can pick it up and make successful use of it immediately.

Of course, you won't be a master carpenter right away, but over time you can master it and find new and other effective uses for it. Who can and should use Buyer Legends?

- **Executives can better communicate strategy from the top down.**
- **Marketers can create and optimize campaigns.**
- **Companies can create and optimize an entire system, like a website, sales funnel, or a complete customer experience.**
- **Managers can optimize cycles and improve execution.**
- **Customer service can optimize customer service channels.**

- **Analysts can interpret analytics and make the case to optimize specific channels and experiences.**
- **Product management can create and optimize products and services.**
- **Content creators and content marketers can plan, optimize, and create more relevant content.**
- **Developers can create and optimize apps and online experiences as well as create buy-in and better communicate with outside teams.**
- **Sales can optimize the sales funnel and create new ones.**

We have been using stories and narratives as a business and marketing tool with our clients for over 10 years, and we are still discovering new uses and creative ways to apply it. If you understand and can demonstrate the relevance of your product or service, you don't need to be a Buyer Legends expert. Buyer Legends is a wonderfully simple concept that can be as robust and complex as needed for the situation. And regardless of that situation, application (even imperfect application) of Buyer Legends will almost always have positive impact. So as you contemplate getting started, be encouraged that it will be hard for you to 'mess it up'. Here's why:

- Firstly, even an imperfectly-constructed legend will stimulate a more intuitive and empathic response in a team. These results in a team that can create more customer-centric touch points and experiences that, in turn, will perform better. Customer insight comes in two forms: intellectual understanding and empathic feeling. By using Buyer Legends to add feeling to the mix, you've essentially doubled

your sensitivity to the customer. That can never be a negative.
- Second, Buyer Legends will focus your team by pointing them all in the same direction and giving them the contextual understanding to unleash their intuition, talent, and initiative to create significantly better marketing with less oversight and half the number of iterations teams normally experience—even when team members come from separate departments and disciplines. This allows for more efficient execution, and gives you the ability to test and optimize customer experiences as a whole instead of in silos.

When it comes to using Buyer Legends as a tool in your organization, we encourage you to just get started, leaving behind the idea of getting it perfect.

# WRITE YOUR FIRST BUYER LEGEND IN 90 MINUTES

The most critical part of the Buyer Legends process is the legend itself. A legend is a story of how and why a customer interacts with your brand. In this section, we will show you how to write your first legend. We will explain how to select your customer's perspective, how to plan and outline your legend, and what elements to include when you write your legend.

To start using Buyer Legends, we recommend you start small by writing a Buyer Legend for a single-content piece - an email, flyer, landing page, or banner ad.

**The exercise of writing your first legend will take approximately 90 minutes.**

    1. **Selecting your perspective** - 15 minutes
    2. **Pre-Mortem list** - 10 minutes
    3. **Reverse chronology outline** - 15 minutes
    4. **Legend draft** - 50 minutes

Almost anyone can write a legend by themselves, but it can also be done as a group. It is usually a good idea to involve anyone on the team who owns the channel metrics for which you are writing the legend. Keep your team small for the first few legends you write, as you become more comfortable with the process you will see opportunities to involve more people.

Also, you should invite Sales and Customer Service in to give you additional first-hand perspectives on how customers are behaving and what they say they need. The best time to invite them in is near the beginning of the process: when you're selecting your perspective and creating a pre-mortem list.

Finally, if getting feedback will be necessary to get buy-in from outside your direct team, share your first draft with those key influencers and decision-makers, so you can make so you can make any needed adjustments before you lock it down.

To begin the process, you must pick your subject/customer who will be the heroine or hero of the Buyer Legend. In other words, you'll need an Ad hoc persona. If your company already uses personas, you can start by using one of them. If you don't have personas, you will need to create an Ad hoc customer persona that reflects a segment of your target audience.

Your Ad hoc persona will supply the perspective for your Buyer Legend, and you can create your persona/select your perspective with the following process:

## 1. Select your perspective:

A. Whose story (or legend) is this? Start with basic demographics, which should be representative of your typical customers, when possible. If you have a broad base of customers, don't worry about representing everyone for now, simply select a common type or segment to get you started. List the traits of your customer and be sure to give him or her a name. It helps to be specific in your list of traits, as you want to end up with something that sounds like a real individual rather than a generalized stand-in. Start with a name and then give them an exact age, a career, a title, even an income if it is relevant to the story. The goal is to make your customer come alive in the reader's mind. While all this may seem a tad superfluous, names and specifics will help you and your readers imagine the persona as an actual person, which in turn, will inspire empathy. Adding a picture of your persona/customer using an image search is also helpful. You can image search on your selected name or on career, etc.

B. Next, consider the buying style of your customer. While there are several buying styles people use, your persona will primarily tend towards one style, especially within the context of this one Buyer Legend. When in doubt, we've found that selecting a deliberate buying style provides the best results for a first-time use. A customer with a deliberate and detail-oriented buying style will, by design, ask the most questions, and because of their penchant for being thorough, will at some time in their journey, reflect many of the other buying styles. This buying style most fears making the wrong decision, and as a result, will ask the most questions. They want to know how it works, why they would benefit from a specific feature, what it can do for them, and what happens if they aren't satisfied? It is likely your company has dealt with these buyers, so get familiar with their needs and questions and integrate them into your legend. Additionally, imagine this customer in the early-buying stage, early enough where they are not even aware of your service and/or product as a possible solution for them.

C. Next, define your conversion goal. Think of this as the destination for this customer's journey. What is the end of the story? Did they buy something? Become a lead? Complete a task? Write it all down.

## 2. Now that you have a perspective/persona, you can begin making a pre-mortem list, detailing the most likely things that could derail this customer's successful journey to your desired destination:

A. Begin by having your Team imagine that the customer has completed her (or his) buying journey and either didn't buy at all, didn't buy what you sell (in favor of an alternative solution), or bought from a competitor. Now ask yourselves:
What went wrong that led to these outcomes?
i. Your intuitions about the most likely bad outcomes and most likely causes will be more insightful than you may think.
ii. This process will give your team permission to voice doubts or fears about your brand's interaction with customers that they might not otherwise feel safe in doing.

B. For every wrong turn, missed opportunity, or bump that could derail the customer's successful journey, take time to imagine how that process would most likely play out. For instance, how would this detail-oriented customer react if a major detail about your product is left out of their journey or if that detail was hard to find? What would that look and feel like, and at what point would that frustration or anxiety actually derail the sale?

C. Now think up fixes, resolutions, and work-arounds for each failure point. The point to the pre-mortem exercise is to give you insight into problems that exist in your current buying paths, so that you can then use it to immunize your conversion funnel from common (and not so common) mistakes that will keep your customer from closing the deal. Understanding these will help you write a more realistic and helpful Buyer Legend when you move onto the next step of Reverse Chronology.

## 3. Outline the story using reverse chronology; start from the end of the story and work backwards. This reverse chronology process will:

A. Ensure your legend ends in success.

B. Emphasize cause-and-effect more effectively than forward chronology, as it will be harder to "fake" or rely upon momentum. Simply by thinking backwards you will naturally be more thorough in defining the actions and reasoning why your customer has taken each step on their journey.

C. Allow you to see and consider alternate, branching paths from your Pre-Mortem list and build in whatever interventions and detours might be needed.

## 4. Now write your Legend draft:

A. Unlike the outline, you want your story to unfold from the beginning to the end. Don't be overly concerned with your writing style, but rather focus on clearly and simply communicating what is happening to your customer as they journey through their experience with your brand. Be as detailed as possible.

B. Here are some additional questions to consider as you write your first draft; what needed to happen to get the customer to complete your goal? What opportunities could you have missed? What loopholes haven't been closed that would hold them back from buying? What opportunities (upsell/upgrade) can we take advantage of? What could you have done to make it easier for the customer along their journey?

Write your legend in third-person omniscient, as this will give you a point of view that allows you to describe the journey in your customer's head and of your campaign in detail.

Ideally, you will include all the following elements in your legend:

**1. A person.** Who is your customer? This can be a persona or an Ad hoc persona that includes relevant customer data and insight into how the customer prefers to make decisions.

2. **The person's purpose.** What are the customer's larger goals? How does she define herself? What is she trying to accomplish on a larger level: career-wise, personally, or socially? In other words, what is the context of her purpose and her motivation? These things will inform her smaller objectives.

3. **The objective of the interaction.** What is she trying to achieve by interacting with your company? What is your conversion goal for this customer at this stage of her buying process?

4. **The sequence of steps in the person's plan.** Tell the story of what the customer is doing at every step of their progress through the sales/conversion process.

5. **The person's rationale behind identifying the problem and executing a solution.** Describe how the customer is thinking before, during, and after each step of the sales/ conversion process.

6. **The key decisions the person will make.** Describe the crucial decisions the customer must make to complete the conversion, and describe what she needs (features, benefits, testimonials, reviews) to make that decision.

7. **The emotional struggles the person might face.** However a person rationalizes a decision, every person makes the decision based on an emotional dynamic. What is the emotional dynamic? Is it a strongly-felt need? Pressure from others? Trust in the brand? Time versus money?

8. **The anti-goals that will put off a person.** What kinds of things must you avoid in this experience? Every person pursuing a goal not only has an objective, they have concerns and anxieties

around what they don't want and don't want to happen. If you don't address these concerns and anxieties, or allow even a hint of possibility that these things might happen, you will jeopardize the sale.

9. **The additional constraints and considerations.** What else does the customer need to consider? Does she have any limitations that may keep her from converting? Can you do anything to address concerns and remove those limitations?

10. **The reasonable alternatives available to the person.**
What other options does the customer have? What kind of experience might she have with a competitor? What if temporary or permanent inaction is a good option?

Please take another look at Vince's partial Buyer Legend. Try to identify which essential elements the story contains. You'll find most of them are included:

> Vince just learned yesterday that Sandy, his bookkeeper of 14 years, is quitting for personal reasons. She'd gone on a two-month leave of absence a few years ago, and it had taken three younger people to semi-competently do her job. A couple of his jeweller friends have suggested he look into an online service to handle his 27-employee payroll.
> Vince likes to call the three stores he has built across Houston Metro his 'jewelry store empire". At 46, he is at the top of his business game, but he is also set in his ways, and must be dragged kicking and screaming to the computer and into the Internet Age. Vince opens his laptop with more than a tinge of resentment. It never takes much for him to get flustered when he is online.

> As he arrives at Steve's company website, he sees faces like his, and reads short testimonials from small business owners. The faces look like the entrepreneurs and business owners he meets and networks with. One of the testimonials tells of a customer's struggle with deployment and how the customer support team had worked closely with his staff to fix the problems. Vince is wise enough to know these types of deployments always have problems, and because the testimonials don't seem to cherry-pick perfect customer experiences, his confidence that this company might be a viable option grows.

Now that your draft is complete, you can begin editing it and revising it for writing style. While it is not necessary for it to read like a Stephen King novel, good pacing and an easy to follow storyline will make your legend much more effective.

Your legend will contain measurable components that can be used to optimize the conversion funnel.

What follows are some crucial definitions we use for measuring legends and a dissection of the process we just described. It will be helpful to review the following sections before starting your own legend.

# MAKING BUYER LEGENDS MEASURABLE AND ACCOUNTABLE

Your hero is on a journey. You tell his or her story. Every successful customer journey needs a map and every map needs a legend. The journey's legend is the key to navigating the map. See below the components of a legend.

## Journey Legend:

**Hero** - This is the protagonist of your legend. All legends are told from the point of view of the hero.

**Catalyst** - This is the point at which the customer first identifies your company, product and/or service as a potential solution. It can be word-of-mouth, on or offline advertis-ing, or PR. A catalyst can be a measurable step in the customer's path, but often cannot be attributed to just one thing.

**First Measurable Step** - This is where your customer enters the measurable portion of the journey. It can be a landing page, home page, chat session, phone call, brick and mortar visit.

Road signs - These are points in the customer's path that are critical to their completion of the journey. Road signs include information that if not available will most likely prevent the customer from completing the journey and/or keep the marketer from persuading them to make a decision necessary to continue on the journey.

Detour - Detours are pathways that marketers must construct as solutions to forks in the road. Customers don't always go straight down a smooth sales path. They often go off the path in search of answers to concerns, alternative solutions, or just plain curiosity. When this happens, the potential exists for that customer to never arrive at your desired destination -- they took that wrong left turn at Albuquerque and never got where they wanted to be. Detours meet the customer along those "wrong turns/paths" and guide them back to the proper path so they can continue their journey to the destination.

Measurable step - Any step that can be measured. Typically this involves analytics, but it is any step a customer can take that leaves behind evidence of that step. Measurable steps give insight as to where customers are in their journey and how they can be optimized.

Fork in the road - These are decision points in the persona's path where a specific need or curiosity can take a customer off the ideal path in search of answers to a specific need, curiosity, question, or concern. Because the marketer should never force a customer down a path, awareness of where a customer could go "off-track" becomes crucial, so that the marketer can plan for these forks in the road and construct detours that will take them from an undesired direction and lead them back to the desired path.

**Destination** - This is the final measurable step where the customer converts into a lead or sale, completing an order, form, or task.

# DISSECTING THE BUYER LEGEND

This legend began by selecting a simple perspective to help our fictional CEO Steve solve the problem of his company's homepage. We chose a thoughtful but determined buying style for Vince, our Ad hoc persona. We made him come to life with specific details about his business and attitude towards it and put him in a situation where he could benefit from Steve's company and services.

If you remember, Steve's observation was that his company was too technical, so for good measure we wrote Vince as a bit of a luddite, knowing that would force Steve's company to consider the needs of a previously-overlooked customer segment.

*(Element #3 - This legend begins with the Ad hoc persona's objective on this journey.)*

Vince just learned yesterday that Sandy, his bookkeeper of 14 years is quitting for personal reasons. She'd gone on a two-month leave of absence a few years ago, and it took three younger people to semi-competently do her job. A couple of his jeweler friends have suggested he look into an online service to handle his 27-employee payroll.

*(Element #6 - We understand that solving his accounting problem is a key decision he will make here.*

*Element #10 - We also learn that Vince has an option of using his existing staff to cover Sandy's work.)*
Vince likes to call the three stores he has built across the Houston metro his 'jewelry store empire'.

*(Element #1 -This paragraph answers the questions "Who is this customer?" Element. #2 You also get an idea of their purpose.)*
At 46, he is at the top of his business game, but he is also set in his ways, and he has to be dragged kicking and screaming to the computer and into the Internet Age. When Vince opens his laptop, it's with more than a tinge of resentment. He hates mouses and clicking, and it never takes much for him to get flustered when he is online.

*(This paragraph also includes Elements #7 and #8; Vince's aversion to technology sets the stage for an emotional struggle [#7], and makes clear that placing complex forms and technology in his buying path is an anti-goal [#8])*

*(Element #4 - we begin to describe his journey in detail)*
As he arrives at Steve's company website, he sees faces like his and reads short testimonials from small business owners. The faces look like the entrepreneurs and business owners he meets and networks with. One of the testimonials tells of a customer's struggle with deployment and how the customer-support team has worked closely

with his staff to fix the problem. Vince is wise enough to know these types of deployments always have problems.

*(Element #9 is Vince's actual IT consideration)* … and because the testimonials don't seem to cherry-pick perfect customer experiences, his confidence grows that this company might be a viable option.

*(Element #5 is pervasive in this paragraph as we get a bird's eye view of how Vince is thinking.)*

**Vince's Ad hoc Persona:**

Persona for: **Steve's SAAS Accounting/payroll business**
Name: **Vince**
Profession: **Entrepreneur. Owns three jewelry stores in Greater Houston metro; has 27 employees.**
Age: **46**
Buying style: **Slightly deliberate and emotional buyer. Smart, impatient.**
Purpose: **To keep his jewelry stores running smoothly.**
Objective: **To replace Sandy, his bookkeeper of 14 years. Open to promoting from within, hir-ing a new employee, or outsourcing a solution.**
Goal for payroll company: **To convert Vince to a lead.**
Challenge: **Vince is technology averse.**

If you are feeling ambitious, it is more effective to write your persona in narrative form like this:

> Vince is a proud entrepreneur who owns three jewelry stores in the Greater Houston Metro and employs 27 people.

*Vince, 46, has just learned that his bookkeeper, Sandy, who has been with him for 14 years, is stepping down . Vince is not confident that he can find someone as good as Sandy and talks to a jeweler friend about his options. His friend tells him he has been having success outsourcing his payroll, so Vince must begin researching the option. Vince considers most purchases carefully and cares about the people he hires to work with his companies. Still — uncomfortable with computers — Vince has little patience with websites and technology in general and needs things simple or he will give up quickly.*

## Pre-mortem list:

- Technical language will scare Vince away by frustrating and confusing him.
- Vince values reality and will not have confidence if he feels he is being sold aggressively or especially if he feels a company's pitch is flowery or falsely positive.
- Vince is a business veteran and seeing young 'unseasoned' faces on the site will cause him to think that this is not a 'mature' solution.

## Reverse chronological outline:

### 1. Vince becomes a lead

    *A.* Form is simple; only a few fields to fill in.
    *B.* Sees that this company will not hard sell or harass him.

2. Vince warms to the company

   A. Testimonials reflect reality and customers talk about how the company dealt with problems and mistakes, not cherry-picked praise testimonials only.
   B. Vince learns that proper deployment is something this company is serious about
   C. Vince sees images that build his confidence, no cheesy stock images of twenty-somethings with cell phones, but of real-life business owners like him.
   D. Vince arrives at the home page.

3. Vince has a problem and seeks a solution

   A. Vince talks to some of his Jeweler friends and learns that he can outsource a solution, if desired.
   B. Vince explores hiring a replacement or promoting from within and is not excited about either.
   C. Vince learns that his longtime bookkeeper of fourteen years is leaving the company and he knows it will be hard to replace her.

It is our hope that you can begin using Legends right away. Like anything new, applying Buyer Legends might feel a bit uncomfortable or awkward at first, but once you have your first "Eureka!" moment or three, and enjoy more wins along the way, it will become a natural process and feel like the most rewarding way to do your marketing.

Best of luck!

If you are interested in learning even more about the Buyer Legend process, we have made the Legend we used to write this ebook available as a free download.

http://www/buyerlegends.com/resources

# A Letter from Jeffrey Eisenberg

Dear Reader,

For almost two decades my brother, Bryan Eisenberg, and I have been recognized by our peers as authorities in marketing optimization, analytics, and customer experience design. We were deeply grateful for all the success, yet we remained disappointed and unfulfilled. Even with two New York Times best-selling books to our credit, we failed to respond effectively to the two most common questions executives ask us, "What is the secret to selling more?" and "Why doesn't my team get it?"

Increasingly, marketers are (or should be) responsible for the entire customer experience across the web, mobile applications and even retail, from attraction through conversion, and on to retention. Great brands, in-depth knowledge of customers, big data sets, and stunning design are indispensable. But they are not sufficient. Buyer Legends tell the stories from your customer's perspective, communicating the context and intent of every touch point, and how every interaction with your company may simply fall short.

In all our years advising clients, we have taught that you need to have the proper mix of multidisciplinary skills: copywriting, testing and experimentation, search marketing, social media, design and layout, psychology, human behavior and persuasion, marketing and branding, sales presentation, usability and user experience, information architecture plus business and web analytics. And then, to truly sell more and market more effectively, you must understand your company's management issues, the organizational challenges, the resource constraints, corporate cultural beliefs, and your personnel limitations. The breadth of business expertise required to succeed is significant; without it, meeting your sales potential is hobbled.

What about the second question - "Why doesn't my team seem to get it?". That question is both easier to answer and, in theory, easier to solve. It lies in the nature of communication. Today's marketer has an over-full plate. There is simply way too much they must focus on. Where do you start introducing balance and productive communication?

In 2006, we released our second Wall Street Journal and New York Times best selling book "Waiting for your Cat to Bark?", in which we outlined a marketing optimization process. The process, among other benefits, is a solution to the communication problem.

In the eight years since, we have worked with companies of all shapes and sizes that possessed varying degrees of talent and competence. We have tried it all, training and encouraging our clients to go deep into the marketing disciplines as well as guiding them through adopting a very robust optimization process.

But what we didn't know early on was how a single piece of that optimization process, what we at the time called scenario narratives, would reveal itself over and over as the 'one thing' that has the largest impact on a company's ability to sell more and effectively communicate their marketing directives to their team.

**We now know that when a company gets Buyer Legends right, everything else seems to fall into place.**

We've seen companies use Buyer Legends to quickly make significant improvements and then move on to other things. But the companies that have continued to thrive and excel at marketing optimization are those that committed to the process long term and absorbed the principles of Buyer Legends into their marketing culture on their own or assisted by our ongoing mentorship. These companies are committed to using the power of story to better understand the customer and plan better customer experiences. Buyer Legends is a process that improves customer-centricity, which improves business success.

The Buyer Legends process is simple, but not easy. The basic ingredients of a Buyer Legend are the same regardless of the team implementing them. If you put the same ingredients in the hands of unseasoned cooks you can certainly eat well, but if the ingredients are in the hands of a renowned chef you not only eat well, you get a fine dining experience.

It is my wish that you take and use our material and then apply the principles of Buyer Legends in your organization. We would love for you to experiment and then share your stories with us. But, if you don't feel like going at it alone, feel free to contact us. We can help.

Sincerely,

Jeffrey Eisenberg
buyerlegends.com

## About Us

Buyer Legends is a Training and Mentoring company started in Summer 2014.

For the better part of two decades *Bryan and Jeffrey Eisenberg* together with *Anthony Garcia* have helped companies like HP, Google, GE Healthcare, Overstock, NBC Universal, Orvis, and Edmunds implement accountable marketing strategies emphasizing optimization of revenue and conversion rates for engagements, leads, subscriptions, and sales.

*Jeffrey Eisenberg,* together with brother and partner *Bryan Eisenberg,* co-wrote marketing-optimization books Call To Action and Waiting For Your Cat to Bark? - both Wall Street Journal and New York Times bestsellers. They also blog at *BryanEisenberg.com.*

We would like to thank *Jeff Sexton, Lisa T. Davis, Noran El-Shinnawy, Craig Mayfield, Michael Drew, Cinde Johnson, Mia Erichson and Roy H. Williams* for all their help with this book.

jeffrey@buyerlegends.com
bryan@buyerlegends.com

**BUYER LEGENDS**

# Endorsements

If there's one thing that marketers need to get better at in the coming year, it's connecting their story to their marketing efforts for a better customer experience. Buyers are going to go on this journey with or without you; failing to delight them along the way can be the deciding factor in whether or not they buy. With the release of Buyer Legends, Bryan and Jeffrey Eisenberg have created the essential how-to guide for storytelling that drives results by showcasing real-world examples alongside a step-by-step process for writing your very own Buyer Legend.

Jason Miller
*Senior Content Marketing Manager, LinkedIn*

It's not an easy sell when pitching your team on a new process, but discovering that Buyer Legends builds upon the work we've already completed made this a slam dunk. Smart and to the point, Bryan and Jeffrey Eisenberg have outlined a simple way to build a story that connects and converts. Get this book and take a major leap forward with a small amount of smart work.

Brian Clark
*Founder, Copyblogger Media*

Incredibly timely and powerful. Buyer Legends is an important read for teams and organizations that want to establish and maintain more authentic and relatable experiences with their customers while helping them define and accelerate their own unique brand story. After all, effective storytelling is what makes brands memorable and this book does an excellent job of making the art and science of good storytelling tangible and do-able.

Ashley Johnston
*Senior VP Global Marketing, Experian*

    The role of a marketer is increasingly to manage the entire customer life-cycle. Legends is a great guide to help your marketing team make the transition and successfully map out every stage of customer engagement. I have applied the Buyer Legends process as the foundation of our content marketing strategy to ensure every stage of engagement is customer driven.

Tami Cannizzaro
*Vice President, Marketing, IBM Cloud*

    *I recently lamented to Bryan Eisenberg that I was finding it extremely difficult to get inside my customer's head in those first crucial seconds after they arrive both on our web landing pages and more importantly into our bricks and mortar showroom. I simply could not put myself into their unknowing shoes. He responded, " I understand Bill, after learning about Buyer Legends, you will." He added that no matter how poorly I constructed a legend, I would gain enormous insights. I have to admit that both of these statements left me with equal amounts of hope and self-doubt. I can report that Bryan's promise rings so true that I'm astounded. Do the work. Then, come join me over here in the enlightened corner of the room.*

Bill Laidlaw
*CEO, 9 Clouds Beds & Mattresses*

    The beauty of Buyer Legends is that it takes all the hard data that some people seek to use and it marries it with all the storytelling and "soft skills" stuff that some other people prefer using, and it makes the case for why you must use BOTH. This book is a powerful tool to instrumenting the soft and for breathing life into the digital.

Chris Brogan
*CEO/Owner, Media Group*

Made in the USA
San Bernardino, CA
28 November 2017